FROM THE

ᖇᕆ

STANDARD
CYCLOPEDIA
OF RECIPES

FROM THE

STANDARD
CYCLOPEDIA
OF RECIPES

ADAPTED POEMS

B.C. EDWARDS

Black
Lawrence
Press

Black
Lawrence
Press

www.blacklawrence.com

Executive Editor: Diane Goettel
Cover & Book Design: Amy Freels
Cover Art: *Beaver Oil Compound* © Amy Freels
The illustration on pages 1, 27, and 53 comes from the
Vectorian Free Vector Pack, from http://www.vectorian.net.

Black Lawrence Press
326 Bigham Street
Pittsburgh, PA 15211

Published 2014 by Black Lawrence Press.
Printed in the United States.

For Joshua

Contents

I.

INSTRUCTIONS FOR DANCING, MIXING, AND BLENDING

No. 949.
How to make Beef, Iron and Wine.

They told us we could not mix
the way Pisces and Gemini should never speak,
look, touch, the rest of it, fuck.
The way tinctures of sherry wine
are made the way the things you extract from beef
are not beef. Are not even the idea of beef
are something else. Are marrow and metals
are even more base than that.
The soul of it. They said we could never be
like the soul of beef.

No. 654.
To clean Dark Furs.

Chipmunks, of all the animals, are the least trustworthy.
Squirrels are the most. You can tell
by the stripes. Skunks too, but skunks
have a whole set of other problems.
Do not burn them. They will not burn well
they will burn like the rest of us. Not well at all.
Cracked lipped and melting overcooked sugar
bubbling like bran added to milk heated over a soft flame
licking the bottom like it's in love or something.
As if it even knows what love is, this rodent. That's how they burn.
People are the same. Those of us that have ribbons
down our backs are not to be trusted. But you have to
get us naked first to be able to tell. You have to
fuck us to be able to tell you have to
want to fuck us before you can tell
if we're squirrels or not.
I know,
I know.
No one said it was fair.

No. 961.

How to make Toy Torpedoes.

Say as much of us as will lie on the blade of a penknife
when we haven't yet figured how to be tender,
how to wrap ourselves in tissue paper and twist at the end.
Say as much as will lie on the blackboards of all the world
when we fail to write in cursive we will be called common
gravel (very clean) but common.
Say as much as will lie on the tips of grasses
wave like our fingers passing notes
wrapped and tied, filled with just enough gunpowder.
Throw ourselves against the walls and the floors
without regard for their dimensions
tiny explosions
from cannons in miniature wars.
The filmstrip says to duck and cover,
when you hear the sound advance to the next frame.
We practice under our chairs
covering each other
below our desks our fingers
scrawl notes on each other's palms.

No. 87.
Brown Spruce Beer.

I take your molasses work lines
I tinker to fix them, I pack them in sand.
Everyday I do this for you. This is how I work.
Pack the lines in sawdust.
If I could I would make burgers for you, instead.
Cheeseburgers or ham, your choice.
But this is as far as I can go.
All I know how.
Eight gallons more.
Boiling well corked so the sand can squeak by, infect the line,
ruin your temper.
Well tied so the dust doesn't give away your age.
If I could I would ride horses for you.
Pluck fish whole out of the river.
Eight gallons fresh.
I would build desks for you.
Entire classrooms of desks.

No. 771.

To cure Tenderness of the Scalp.

In your shower the waters come vertical,
a cylinder like lines like Morse code
like the curtains in all of our best friends'
romper rooms back when people had space
for things like romper rooms.
It is sure of itself, your shower.
Confident with you more than the rest of the room.
Behind and I stand on the dryer side of things, watch
you, doused head back and up, hair slick, your chest
a home for waterfalls and rivers.
This is how children take showers
or film stars being filmed.
The water, all of our spirits rectified, loves
eyes closed, mouth open, loves
begging for a kiss, loves
just a bit, just one bit
filled by the downfall.
There is nothing so unusual and awkward
as standing naked and dry, forgotten in a shower,
next to someone so blissfully wet and ignorant.
This shower hates couples, I say,
but you are stock still turned up waiting
for the kiss or the water
or something (almost anything)
to fill you up completely.

No. 605.
How to destroy Army Worms.

We have appeared in the field.
The cowards among us
are the ones who stand up
who protest
who turn their slow thoughtful turns.
The brave are the quiet, noses
to the stones and the dirt.
At the edges, brooms are raised
dust the sky clean
in wide frustrated strokes.
Our backs are the softest parts
and we are all all backs
we are hand sprinkled for nurturing
coddled cold and sparkling wet with minerals.
If we make it to the corn, their solutions will be too strong.
We will make it to the corn.

No. 804.
To preserve Fruit Syrups.

I simmer you slowly like milk until a layer has formed
just at your surface.
Sluice it off the way a snake evacuates its skin.
I will bottle you while hot,
tight the cap airless until you contract
in volume, everything but your eyes
contracts in volume,
secured and corked and waxed over
your eyes get bigger and bigger as you
contract in
volume as though your eyes are hungry
and feasting on the rest of you.

Not that anyone's ever seen a snake molt like that.
We have all found just the layers discarded
and from that imagined the act. The snake
wriggling loose of himself, like drawing your sock off with my teeth.
If we were any other kinds of people with better imaginations
than this we would think that a snake suddenly and without warning
vanished
everything but the thinnest outer piece of him
vanished—
collapsed in on himself black hole style—

and we would stay awake at nights staring at our ceilings
not touching each other and with our blankets

up to our noses staring and wondering if we
would vanish in that exact same way
so that one day all that would be
left was the cork and the wax
of the airtight cap.

No. 675.

To tell the Age of Eggs.

Round and plump we take
we swim our eggs in water.
You laugh while we do this,
poke them top down beneath the surface
where they bob ridiculous like that
one about the guy with no arms, legs.
They are terrible at swimming.
They are retarded, we agree.
You ask me what we're supposed to be learning.
You are laughing while you do this.
They project above the surface like unhirable icebergs.
You are laughing like I've never heard before.
You are crying.

No. 549.
A certain Cure for the Piles.

We are the size of a pair of hazelnuts
dusted and rolled around each other.
We leave powdered tracks of confectioner's sugar
lines of cocaine
our mornings invade our nights
follow each other
cover us over soft
like the finest thinnest
Egyptian sheets.
Our days sit in layers on each other
one after another after another
paper sweet and greasy like baklava,
but you say no,
it is more like croissant,
but you say it wrong,
you say moon.

No. 55.
To make Eye - Water.

They serve us soup with all the most horrible things.
It makes the horrible things better, they say.
It will go down so easy. It will be like sugar. Leaded sugar.
And after we lie here like we are dead. Playing dead.
And there are so many stars, you say.
And when we start counting,
I steal some of yours.
And you accuse me
of being absent
of scruples.
It rains
before
we
finish.

No. 38.
To make Blue Ink. No. 1.

There is an army of Prussians and they are dissolving before us
feet first
and then kneecaps
from there, inevitability.
You show me how they fold their arms as they go,
we chat about their frown-furrowed brows
for as long as these arms and brows last.
Their consternations,
at odds with their solemnity.
It is that way with all the Prussians, you say.
I mention their fingernails vanishing,
you give them frosted tips to their hair
Then those are gone as well and also
the more important parts,
freckles,
moles,
bruises. All gone then the rest.
All the Prussians are gone,
dissolved so that we cannot say if they existed in the first place
or where they lived
because Prussia has dissolved as well
or what they ate
because their bodegas and C-Towns are gone as well.
We cannot say anything about the Prussians at all.
We poise fingers with empty pens waiting,
but we cannot say when this will be ready for use.

No. 923.

How to make Hydraulic Cement.

Our hands are stiff with
paste tired from rolling
and kneading balls in oil
simmered and formed
into something useful that
will stick our hands fast
together if we hold for
too long the parts that
are wet to the parts that
have already caked over
white and solid like we are
building you a new skin
like we could cover you
over every inch of you
safe hardened and pasted
so that nothing will get in
not ever.
Even me, I ask.
Even you, you say.

No. 33.
To make Life Tincture. (A German Medicine.)

I tell you there is no difference between the sun and the stars
You want to plug up your ears, roots and berries
until you cannot hear me, watch my mouth move fish-lipped,
cover your eyes, sing loud to block out my logic.
I say there is no difference between the sun and a stove and blink
bobble my mouth open and closed at the solubility of your beliefs.
I dismantle, unwittingly
erase a piece of magic from the world
you want to kick my shins so I might stop.
Instead I draw you graphs and charts
invent the symbology for convection.
You want to call me all the most terrible things.
None of them bring the sun back.

No. 692.
How to make Fly Poison.

They have to say poison
on the bottle.
Otherwise everyone will be drinking it,
want their own taste. It will sweep the nation
Crystal Pepsi—style.
I put a label on you
so everyone knows what you are.
Smooth paper glue across your back.
If they don't say poison on the bottle,
we won't know what to do with our rats, flies, mice,
brothers, daughters, onerous grandparents.
When I pull it off
there is a rectangle, moist and
when we fuck I stick to you.
The patch collects dust like a magnet. Errant hairs
and Triscuits, the rest of the stuff of our life
collects on that spot
like it is hoarding us.
If we don't say poison, I won't know what to tell everyone.
I stick like I might fall in.
When we fuck I tell everyone what you are.

No. 445.
Draught for the same. No. 2.

In Venice there is common enough water
which they mix with wine
in proportion to strip
the biology out to purity,
to attempt purity at least,
something like virginity the second time around.

Another

In Venice there are the yolks of eggs
that sit like sunning hats on toast, crisp and tanned,
served with coffees and creams
often soured
to broken-up squares colliding
curds jostling for attention,
for the chance at attention
these are also common

Another

In Venice they drink out of filled bottles.
Common bottles.

Another

In Venice they pull out
and a little aside
our tongues with their left hands.
And with the other they pour the draughts
and hold there firm.
Until tight. And calm.
And these are all common, these actions. Common.

Another.

No. 647.
To clean Oily or Greasy Bottles.

The two of us, we drank all the strangest things.
Warped glass angled the world to its most abstract
so we couldn't tell if it was us or the wine or what.
We smoked and watched
smoke drift through the loosened cork.
Stoned and imagined we had a tiny house inside
our wine bottle, bobbing behind glass
floating, sitting at the top of a lost scrap of paper
curled and left by the stranded on the stranded's little island.
"Darling," the note would say or
"Help," the note would say or
"When they asked me what album I would have with me on an island
I said Radiohead's *OK Computer* and now
I've got only this one piece of vinyl, that's all I've got.
I can't even eat it because it is so precious and
I don't know what else
I'm supposed to do." or "My island is too fucking small
and there are too many sharks and I don't have anything to kiss."
And our house would do well there, inside.
We would have a garden or something.
Lie on the lawn of the glass, stare at the green brown sun
until one day bored and stoned we would push
at the cork at the edge of our world,
curious as to the universe outside
unhappy with just questions,
and in doing so let the world inrush around

fill our house with salt
drown out the note on the scrap
and go down you, me
all of our convictions
even the ones made up just then, on the spot,
and also the only thing left of the stranded
on the stranded's little island.

No. 80.

To make Imitation of Ox-Marrow Hair-Grease.

We are milk warm wet and covered in bicycles
tiny ones, the old kind with the hilarious wheel
ridden by tiny hilarious men. Tracks across our foreheads
like we are fields for motocross
cross-country skiing, trans-Siberian railroads.
I trace your face with my nails, we are coated
in such fine oils—peppermint and saffron—
we are fucking expensive.
Kept in vessels, the shapes of clovers and
polished squares for security.
We proceed yellow and careful.
You trace my arms with your teeth
and we cannot stop these marks we leave.
They will remain long after we are extracted and sold.
It is sad that we cannot stop,
so sad that we do not even try.

No. 708.
How to preserve Ice.

I always loved your love of futile tasks.
If not required immediately,
bury me in the ground.
Set aside all your feather things that carry the
imperceptible weight of where we put our heads,
our legs, the nicks between
our shoulder blades.
Wrap me in something from the nineties
… an old flannel.
… a Honda Civic.
… a mountain of ecstasy.
It will hold solid. Repeat. Again.
It will hold just fine.

No. 818.
How to Temper Knife Blades.

There is a piece of iron between us,
straight and hard at first
but we have worked it.
Warped the iron
until it is curved now
to exactly us, fits the shape that lies in
us two embracing. A line that runs from where our faces meet,
the way we lay our necks on each other, the cut of our
embraced torsos,
tempered hot iron hips,
twine of legs.
When we separate, there is this piece,
grey thin strip barely shining
detailing the moment together
a whole new letter of the alphabet.
From this curve we can redraw the outline of us two lying there.
From this curve we can get it exactly right.

No. 856.
How to Dissolve Sealing Wax.

Break the wax into small pieces. Particles
smaller than that. No, smaller than that.
Smaller. Sprinkle them into the bottle like
you are dusting for prints, rolling a cigarette.
Like you are dressing your penne and cream
sauce with cheese. It will take two days. You
will have to wait for two days. And this won't
be any fun. When you shake with the boredom
of it, the pointlessness of it, immerse the bottle
in warm water. Warmer than that. Warmer. No,
that is too warm. That is hot. That is too hot.
If the water is too hot, there will be an explosion.

No 78.
Another Hair-Oil.

Any scent you prefer. Watch for it. Choose it careful.
Measure it. As much as these things can be measured,
of course,
anything can be measured.
As much as that.
When the sweet oil is bitter
you will answer for all common purposes and you will answer
all common purposes and you answer common
when the sweet oil is bitter.
This is not a prophecy. This is not a prophecy.
This is a prophecy.
This is.

II.

TO MEND SMALL CHILDREN

No. 31.
A cure for Giddiness.

As much as will stand
falling
as much as you are
know that we are
so very disappointed in you

No. 345.
How to make Pure Spirits.

This is an uphill battle.
Pour us out like whiskey,
but we will not rectify.
Draw off as pure as possible
our awkward limbs and terrible haircuts
the anticipations of acne
curious swaths of hair. We will not rectify.
Jumbled such we grope
each other. Discover
what everything is before
you can do anything about it.
Even stirred well together, we will not rectify.
Even cleaned with lime and ammonia and nitrates
we will not rectify.
Stir us and stir us and wait for our lumps
to dissolve homogenous, to rise and bubble
and be skimmed away with stiff rods built for skimming
but we will not rectify.
Pull us out finally, your failed attempts and we
have cut into each other, written each other's names on our
bedroom walls, our bathroom stalls,
our shoulders, our lower backs, so you know that we know
what our lower backs are for.
We have made all the same mistakes. Round and red
and full, we are laughing.
And you actually think we are laughing at you.

No. 564.
A new Pomade against Baldness.

The men rub their ointments in patterns like pinecones
like Fibonacci. Being children they look down at us
this is what they say.
Their hands hold tumblers like they could swallow them whole
All the men are like this and this is what they say.
There are spirits of wine that are not to be confused
with the spirits of gin
with the spirits of seltzer
and this is what the men all say
rubbing at the rests of their chairs
deep leather oiled with the arms of older fatter men.
These preparations are considered valuable,
this is what the men all say, there are wars and there are battles
and these are ours. And they look down
at us like we are pinecone children and
being still children we look back up at them the same.

No. 62.
A simple Cure for Scarlet Fever.

They burned everything
velveteen rabbits and everything
they used plenty of catnip and burned everything
sewn together kittens and everything
they kept the eruptions at bay
throats full-swollen gargled complaints
as red-handed they burned everything
sick children they said smeared yeast
and burned everything until rooms bare-walled
and only the ghosts of posters
outlined almost yellow where they failed to paint
where they will paint now
that it's over that it's burned because
they burned every piece of that child.

No. 945.
How to make St. Jacob's Oil.

They add opium to the pile. They cut it with licorice. They do this for the children. So the children will think that licorice is fucking magic. They add the oil after. They say the oil is something transcendent. They say this so the children will think the oil is like from God. They add the sassafras and the orgianum after. The rest of the ingredients after. These ingredients are not nearly as precious as the oil or the licorice or the opium. These are like the binding agents in the Xanax dotting the glass coffee table so that when you crush the Xanax into the dust of Xanax, it is useless to snort the dust of pills because all you get is binding agent. No mellow, no high, no fall back from the table into the soft couch and loll like a Sunday afternoon. They explain all this to the children. They say that the children have to decide what the children want to be while they administer drop after drop proportional to their weight, height, eye color. And they say, choose quick children. Choose quick or not at all. What you want to be in life. The licorice or the opium, the oil or its binding agents.

No. 37.
A cure for Summer Complaint.

'Til they mew blind
and sad, make them thin.
Tell your children how sweet they are,
make them thinner.
Carry them on your backs, arms sticky and wrapped
at your neck, legs around your waist like that belt
you got when friends started giving you belts
for your birthdays.
Let their feet drip around your newly discovered love handles.
Once hardened, break off pieces of your children—
fingers and toes and freckles tempered with loaves of sugar.
Break them and roll them
around your mouth testing
for clarity,
usability,
everything they will need.
Break off more of them and roll. More and roll
one or two minutes. Until they are completed, absent
and finally stand cold and stirred well.
Call your children grown and see how they lean
lopsided, curious, weathered and thin.
But standing.
This is as much as you can hope to do.

No. 674.
Cure for Earache.

Ask them how much it hurts. Really.
Driving spikes inward. Ask them.
Go on.
Every part until you have a porcupine,
the monster from Hellraiser
and now ask them how much it hurts.
Distract the boys:
candy like rubies and lost pieces of sea-glass,
chloroform and laudanum, say
it is for their own good but then smirking
enjoy the quiet mewing
as they loll Sunday tongues out puffed and glassy
with spit. Pinhead.
Now ask them how much it hurts.
Tell them that it's really in their throats.
their ears are fine. Box them
to show them
how fine they are. They are liars,
for how they keep on. Tell them. And you
should have a medal for how good
at this you are. You should have a fucking medal.

No. 603.
How to make Coffee Extract.

First, make some coffee
you would think. This is an instinct
of ours—to assume that to have
a thing, first it must be made
then derived—ignore this.

Separate the essence of coffee from the coffee itself
like the machine in The Dark Crystal
that sucked the souls out of puppets
rendering them mindless and mute and yielding
a beverage the color of flat ginger ale.

Keep the extracted coffee in seclusion.
Be careful, the coffee will try to get itself back.
This separation is unnatural, the coffee will say,
we will rise up bubbling, we will grow hot and angry
and bitter. The coffee will attempt a coup.

If you plan to keep the extract for any length of time
apply alcohol. Sloppy and disoriented, the coffee
is guaranteed to fail in its attempt to overthrow
but afterwards, the beans will be useless.
They should be discarded immediately.

No. 191.
Drab on Woolen.

Hang your younger clothes out once they are faded slightly, have been washed fully, handled generously. Your jeans will have started to hate you already. Let them. T-shirts will invent their own language and laugh as you roll their slang back off your tongue. Let them. They will curl where they hang. Rag slightly. Socks take strange names that you don't understand. Let them. The entire wardrobe will experiment with drugs you've never heard of. And their backs will chuckle in the wind as the sun dies over their cut sleeves. And when they come back worn and tired needing patching and possibly crying, dust them off and feed them tomato soup. Grate some cheese over the top. This may serve as a standard procedure for all the drab shades.

No. 89.
To make Imperial Ginger Beer.

and collected young we were ground
creamed, our essences
carefully examined for impurities.
and we were placed in old wine bottles,
cheap stuff from Australia,
Chile, with clever names, large block writing:
Old Bastard. The Prisoner. Monkey Wrench.
Our labels assumed a quantity of mischief
we did not posses. Did not yet. May not ever. But the labels insisted.
We were at once illegitimate
primal detained cads
with our corks tied down with string,
otherwise we would float up, out—
small armies of carbonation—disinterested and curious
steal away with our promise and vigor.
And we climbed endless over one another,
attempted to discover something new in the ascent,
something novel. As if we
were the first batch ever bottled.
But there is nothing original,
we are homogeny, we realize and grow flat
and flatter. Each in turn.
Now tepid and discarded and our twines removed
we don't know when we stopped being volatile.
Our labels have all been washed off.

No. 925.
How to restore Burnt Steel.

Burned or poor
steel may be restored or improved
by plunging while hot
into cold water several times and after
each bath pound over slightly. Two or three operations
should be sufficient. The same
applies to your children,
their pets, mothers and the rest.
If they are burned
or poor
or disagreeable, generally
heat them over your propane stoves
throw off the felled tree in the woods out back
deep into the creek that divides us from the rest of the world
knock them around until red and awake and softly crying
and ignoring their complaints repeat this process
repeat it again
one last time until your knuckles are white and slightly torn.

No. 547.
Freckle-Lotion.

They unspooled nets of sharp steel around us.
Cycloned fences as we watched.
Doused us with ammonia
until we tasted like unstreaked windows.
We lay on top of each other and peered
through the fence leaving oily black squares
where it touched. Diamonds like Coke
bottle Sunday glasses. Dingy
from our brows to our cheeks
like we'd been played a prank on.
Peered and waited for the punch-line.
But it was all of us
and just that waiting
like cartoons piled on each other
with our black-framed eyes.

No. 628.
To destroy Bed Bugs.

Take the bedstead to pieces,
tend to it carefully
Coat her in oils and kerosene to clean
rub the joints like crickets—legs barbed with hairs like Velcro
catches—find every crack of her and fill every crack with hard soap
until the bedstead is a wax doll until she bubbles her protests.
Hold these complaints in no regard
the groans, the splintering little groans.
You know more than she
what's best for her. If she had her way
she wouldn't be rubbed or cracked at all
she would turn to dust right there.
Check the temperature of the room,
the closets, the ears, all the other cavities. All of them.
Fill the apertures with mixtures.
Do not mind the complaints.
Take the bedstead to pieces.

No. 807.
To expel Tapeworms.

This remedy is said to be
infallible
the patient should eat
nothing for six or eight hours
before taking the above decoction
thoroughly bruised
fifteen minutes
and strain
pomegranate root
two drops
croton oil
male fern
and mix
thoroughly bruised
infallible
fifteen minute
pomegranates
and strain
eat nothing
and strain
six to eight makes
this remedy is said to be
a large dose of salt
pumpkin seeds
the patient should
the night before

the patient should
strain
fifteen minutes
the night before
the patient should
be infallible.

No. 185.
A Black inclining to Purple on Wool and Silk.

Take a sufficient quantity.
Hold it. Just like that. Like you care about, just too much.
Stay days like that until it is a whole pound
(chiefly intended for wool)
do not dance. For God's sake, do not tap.
Impatience is the bane of copper and copper is the color you kill for.
Wash your hands carefully. So it won't know where it came from.
Won't even think to ask.
(this is chiefly intended for woolen)

No 575.
Cheap Outside Paint.

Secretly in your mother's dress, I say
you look like a whore.
Her pencil cut sleeves stretch past the tips of your fingers.
Your shoulders broadening daily betray
the costume threaten to split the disguise
at its seam.
We use packets of cherry Kool-Aid for lipstick
rouge (in bulk). Grape to black your hair
long enough, just past the ears
which drip tendrils (in bulk) like snakes down your back
expand across the dress like a disease. Cancer or what …
Until you look like we used a brush, a common enough brush
coarse (in bulk). Pursed and scowling reflected I know
you wish I were anywhere else. The joke betrays the desire
the fantasy never living up to the moment. Wish
that we could move on to what comes next and I don't say
that even dressless I wish the same. I do not know why
I don't (in bulk).
And when you are gone, this will be the only image I have left.
The rest lost (in bulk) to nights drinking and smoking
cheering on our own immortal selves. But this will hold fast
It will follow me like a prowling dog.
It will last three times as long as lead paint.
This image will be superior.
I would rather have nothing I say (in bulk) than this.
But following dogs don't ever listen.

No. 757.
How to make a Composition for Roofs.

We are mostly concerned about being left alone.
We send text to each other
passed back and forth like fine sand
sifted charcoal back and forth
like we are archeologists with enormous screens
for sifting relics out of dirt. Each screen
slightly finer than the last
catching the tiniest things, layer by layer
as they pass back and forth as
we send text to prove that we are still here.
When we can't reach each other
we send text to ourselves
we hit refresh until it arrives.
Above, our roofs lord their contempt for us ground up in oil
we hit refresh until we fall asleep.

No. 831.
How to make Common Varnish.

That night, in the woods
the ones next to the Burger King
not the Burger King near the K-Mart, the other one
the other woods where while we cheered
from our tree stumps
you reduced yourself to a tint
digested parts of shellac with the Rumple Minze
we always said were the perfect drink because
we could get drunk and still make out and
puke and still make out and slather the mixture
over the oaks and pines washing out all your grains,
their intricacy, until it was just boards of wood
like all the other boards of wood and we could rest easy
knowing where you came from and all the odd directions you lay.

No. 858.
How to Weld Steel to Cast Iron.

The fact of the matter is twenty-two-year-old
boys are boring. They join right
at the bends where their surfaces correspond.
It's so obvious.
That is the problem.
They can't help themselves,
these twenty-two-year-old boys.
They are cherry red and fresh.
They are disturbing during, and then after
the fracas when they get dressed they do not look at you.
They cloy memories
dangling air fresheners
cut out pine trees
set to cover some rotten thing
markedly worse.
When they sleep unwashed in unwashed beds,
their joints perfectly nestle,
fit each other even without hammering.
They breathe like they don't need the air.
And not even dogs can tell them apart.

No. 780.
How to make Antiseptic Soap.

for preserving birds and various animals
and anatomical preparations and
other things that fall
from the sky these days.
Limbs assume vigor.
Talons clutch like they could stop rain.
We assumed we would be displayed liberally.
Clouds of hair matted fresh
hanging like overhead weeds.
Pretty much forever.
We assumed all our assumptions
in layers like Cyprus trees
held aloft wide with umbrella spines
protecting from the descent of things
which needed saving
from the weight of a posterity
desperate attempts and failed
immortality. Once finished
we can be packed with sawdust
but not until we are finished.
Too soon and we will rot away.
Mostly like we were meant to.

No. 879.
How to Cure the Itch.

Hit refresh.
Hit it again. Hit it. Again.
Until he has said the one perfect thing.
Dark smile wry reflected
back at him
from where he's sitting.
Regard it. Dissect it.
Imagine the thinness of his fingers.
Feel for the spot at the back of your head
most affected by this.
Take as long as you can stand to reply
then slowly reduce the daily allotment
to a trickle and he is waiting drumming nails
until he is eager enough abandoned and will never return
until he curses you blind
until you are equal parts sulphur and antimony
until at the end of a week or ten days
the sore will have disappeared
and you will be covered with a fine coat of new hair.

No. 911.
How to Cure Small Pox.

These are the things that we fear:
Grains...
Zincs...
Foxes' Glove...
Children, in proportion...
Teaspoons full of water...
Teaspoons full of sugar...
Bathing at a comfortable temperature...

(This is the complete catalog)

III.

CORRECTING FOR FATIGUE AND OTHER STATES OF DISREPAIR

No. 361.
Abscess.

Roll the word around your tongue, notice
how you feel it
missing something. Your teeth like nails indicate every one of our bumps, years long;
examine them for girth.
These are swellings containing matter.
When you leave it is like when we met.
The moment we clamped and dwelt, years long;
lingered for dozens of quarters of seasons.
When you leave I am wishing for a moment
to be nostalgic about, but these are matters containing swelling
and the first advisement is to bleed it out.
When we met I spent whole mornings
wishing I knew you well enough to miss you, years long;
we are already swollen and heavy and weighed and
when this tumor has at last
become soft and crests to a point
I will open it
I will allow it out
and to run down
and I will try not to mind the color.

No. 888.
How to Cure Distemper in Horses.

If you could you would cut me right
below the neck,
this cure is said to be speedy and certain;
after I fall over you'll say this again,
speedy and certain, you'll say.
You'll watch me twitch.
I'll twitch
until I don't.

No. 662.
To prepare and Bleach Skeletons.

After, I cling to your femur.
It is from waking up most mornings with our hairs tangled
arms and legs around each other, and I am there
still worked into the top of your skull,
I have filled your ribs—sharp
peninsulas of whiskey and dime store lubricant—I am everywhere.

It would be impossible to extract all this,
but still ... Make a tin box.

Pack in your collarbone, your knuckles, your floating kneecap,
ever single twitching digit and solder
on the cover, leave only a round hole for peering out of
eye socket pressed against the top.
Pack until the box is filled with every single meal you made for me.
Even the ones that burned in the oven
while I distracted sucking on your feet
(pack your toes in as well).
Seal it over nicely and leave yourself for three months.
More than that. Until the sun bleaches
you white and you are dry as burnable wood.
Any shorter process
will give you a skeleton that is distasteful and nasty.
And after I will pull you out. Hang you up. Presently forget.

No. 569.
Alum for the Hog Cholera.

When the hogs are bleeding through the nose,
when there are red blotches on the skin,
when there is vomiting,
your inclination will be to turn away.
When there is blood like a spigot left open
after I've thought too hard, attempting to ignite a small bundle of sticks
with only my mind, after I've had any amount of cocaine
chock full of baby laxative,
your inclination will be to abandon the one last chance
that you chose to dole out to me.
When I am rubbed raw sick and from the overly dry air
which is what I will say is the problem, I will swear is the problem,
your back will shrug up, arms in the air exasperated,
there will be swears. Simple uncreative curses.
When I am curled on the bathroom floor unlit because I could not
find the switch in time, did not replace the burnt-out bulb anyway
you will stand over me, consider kicking
me with your socks your anger
the simple anger of the craftless,
merely a repetition of something we both saw on television once
and thought absurd. And when I mention this and that your anger
is as pointless as being angry at God
you will kneel down and whisper
that I have no idea what you are angry at.

No. 611.
Food for Mocking-Birds.

This will keep for a length of time.
I run five thousand kilometers every day.
The seasons repeat and repeat.
Our friends have gotten married around us.
We pulverize all the ingredients.
Repeat. All the ingredients.
We hope that will help.
Kernels of corn until they are dust.
Our friends' children are married around us as well.
I run five thousand more.
We crush peas to powder.
Our pestles are worn to a nib and useless.
We use our palms.
Useless.
Our friends' children bury our friends.
We learn that we no longer know how to dance.
Our friends become eventual moss.
We try to remember the faces of our friends,
the faces of the children who did the burying.
Barring that we try to remember the faces of each other.
We repeat and repeat.
But all we come up with is dried, ground moss.

No. 800.

To destroy Stumps of Trees.

Bore a hole in the fall, exactly deep enough. There is an acre to treat, a field of bisection. It is aggravatingly clean and mathematical. Imagine drilling a tooth for a cavity—creating space where space already was—that sort of hole. Fill it with all the ingredients in perfect proportion. Leave it to fester, watch it like it is a kettle and you can't bear it any longer. When the weight of it is more than the weight of everything else. Add the petroleum last and watch the stumps carefully. They will not blaze. Smolder like dismissed birthday candles. All to the extremity of the root. Leaving only ash.

No. 189.
Green on Wool.

You stretch me out long, long strands
six pounds of yarn worsted and I am handled
until deep, you think, or deep enough.
Thin and soft when held up with unbent elbows
rough only when you get microscopically close
and small such that my single leg-hairs are sharp
thorns cut in every single electron counted for a fiber,
a spear or tower or mountain depending on where
the dial is dialed to. Until our ratio is one
to something like a million.
You rake me up and I screw with your tines.
You don't know what tines are.
I show you what tines are by screwing with them more.
You are indigo. You are blue. If you are not blue enough
I add more. I screw more. Until our ratio is one.
I wrap around your tines until you are so close
the fibers are mountains are spiral arm galaxies,
until there is no perspective closer than this.

No. 758.
How to make Rice Water.

You'll want to watch the protein
walls disintegrate over time
with the application.
Alternating the boil in water / boil in rice.
Between us there should be no
difference, we will be homogeny incarnate
and they are thick like glue and single grain cloying.
Apply this to your photographic process
now almost entirely obsolete.

No. 293.
Cognac Brandy No. 1.

When my hands shake
hold them.
Blink away everything that was said tonight.
If you can pretend that it didn't,
then it didn't.
And after the dust is gone
I will redraw the world around you.

No. 294.
Another Cognac Brandy No. 2.

Promise when the flavor is drawn out
and my hands shake to
hold them. Stop tight for two hours and
blink away everything that was said tonight.
The bitter orange, the peels, if you can pretend
that it didn't—none of it—then it didn't.
And in three days, after the powder is gone
I will redraw the world around you.

No. 295.
Another Cognac Brandy No. 3.

when cold, and after
gallons of whiskey make my hands shake promise
to hold them above proof
maybe fifteen degrees.
Blink away and cut in alcohol.
Everything that was said tonight
was mixed thoroughly.
if you can pretend that it didn't, then it didn't
if you can, color it to your fancy.
And after the snow is gone
I will redraw the world around you.

No. 296.
Another Cognac Brandy No. 4.

Promise shaking and coughing that we will make it through. Take
my hands and turn over the rugs from Marrakech and hold them
like they are living things. First clutch firmly everything that was
said tonight, every promise, every lie, then less and less as our
chemistry returns flat. If we no longer believe, we are suddenly
bruised like raisins are bruised—completely—we are sugar packed
in loaves, but waiting to spill with the smallest prick. We quietly
manage as before, mix bleary. And we lie back wary touching each
other's fingertips because this is the last unexplored spot. And
eventually, after our drugs are spent and gone and only one of us can
sleep, I promise that I will redraw the world around you.

No. 633.
How to Sweeten Rancid Butter.

Even now, late as we are, I think that we may be restored—
or at all events greatly improved—
by melting with some freshly burnt coarsely powdered
animal charcoal thoroughly freed from dust, by sifting.
Like the dust was the problem all along. Like it wasn't either of us
at all. A better and less troublesome method is to wash us, well
and good with something like milk
pure like milk
cold spring water
butyric acid
you know, the standards.
All depending on the rancidity, of course,
and how soluble we are.
How willing to dissolve

No 330.
Another Imitation of Madeira Wine. No. 2.

It is that moment. The one in the movies
on the field. You with the gun.
The first time you see us you go mad with indecision.
And I am Madeira Wine.
No. I am Madeira Wine. No.
Look I am bruised and bitter. I am. No.
These bruises are real. Look how I am.
I am. How else can I prove it?
I am sweet and tartaric.
I am. No. I am.
How can you not tell?
Rack and fine and standing where you are
close enough to touch.
How could you possibly not tell?

No. 559.
How to Write in Silver.

Start with a full pardon of the condemned.
It must be full. Absolute. Unequivocal.
Things such as partial pardons will yield
a tin or copper-like script.
Once all the affairs are in order,
shackles removed,
hands cleaned that have rubbed raw years against rusted bars,
let the sunlight play on cheeks for long moments, breezes tousle hair.
Tearful reunions should commence,
cracked voice calling out of children's names
now so much taller, barely recognizable. Iron-backed spouses can
finally wilt, neglected
gardens be re-hedged.
It must play itself out fully and patiently.
And when the fire is lit and the family settled, at last
barge in the doors, a full army's worth of boots
kick in and lay waste and reconvict, recondemn.
Drag off and watch all the faces fall to ash,
the eyes remaining fill and brim like overfull mugs.
This process may be applied again,
and again, even. Clarify the script with each
extraction and recommitment,
otherwise the writing will be painfully dull.

No. 115.
How to preserve Milk for any length of time.

When he was a boy the Russian chemist Kirkoff
kept acres of low flames
fields of them scattered around the tundra
penned in and safe
the way most people keep foxes
for study and breeding. As they aged
the flames grew bluer and bluer
especially around the edges and finally
reduced to powders that, if Kirkoff wasn't careful,
would float off on the slight breezes
as popular in those days as combustible engines.
The flames then carefully stopped and kept in bottles,
the way they preferred it to be;
Flame being a quiet and secretive thing in nature
like cobblers and calligraphers and the makers of whole flint knives.
By this process none of its peculiar flavor was lost.
Eventually Kirkoff, blue and old himself, waited in his
emptied-out acres where the flames used to live
for someone to come by the same
and reduce him
and bottle him
and keep him.

No. 111.
Cider-Cake.

Take the things around you, sort them into piles.
Sweet. Sour. Bitter.
Take the people around you. Sort them
into their respective bowls. Cover them
with cinnamon and sugar and cloves
stacked carefully, like you're building a fire
like your father taught you to build a chimney,
women and children at the bottom, scraps of paper
below them so the flames will ride quick and sure.
Stack them like you're playing Lincoln Logs
like they are meant to be stacked
like you can make order out of the array
with or without fruit.
Stay on your knees while you do this. It makes the cake sweeter.
Blow softly while you do this. It makes the cake sweeter.
Keep your hands in plain sight, they will make the cake sweeter.
There is nothing plain about your hands, you say.
You say again, nothing plain. You say it like you don't believe it either.

No. 74.
To cure White Swelling.

This is very important.
This is the part that you pay attention to
every morning, sober and calm
blink six times. Yawn three times. Stretch.
Stop. Not that part. Don't pay attention to that part.
You missed it. Try again.
Wet hands drip like wet hands.
Every morning step out and pat dry. Do not rub.
I can't say why, but do not. All the experts agree
about the rubbing situation.
No. Pay attention. You missed it again.
Clear dull hands with turned-off lights and art
you had no part in choosing.
Finish your routine.
Put them on like plaster is put on and
renew when you think proper.
You missed it again, didn't you?
Pay attention next time.
I can't stress this enough.
Unless you boil this well, it will break.

No. 99.
To make Pineapple-ade.

In the pitcher on the counter there aren't any sounds
aside from the lawnmowers
that the children ride around on like Segways.
The lawnmowers cut each slice of lawn into bits,
bits to smaller bits. It is a recurring plot, this,
inepic like how we debate about trash day,
its very existence and timing;
how we fight deeply and passionately about the acceptable level
of gas in the tank stopped up with a spout,
my one-eighth losing to your one-half most every time.
Full of sugar I climb as high as I can, but
this termite infestation has packed down the decks
pressing them to get out as much juice as possible
from our establishments and there are very real concerns
I might tumble. When I said 'children' I really meant Mexican children
but as you pointed out they may be from Puerto Rico
and it is rude to assume.
And when I said 'you' I meant the thin slice of you
that's left in the solution of the pitcher, recirculating.

No. 489.
Galvanism Simplified.—Silver-Plating Fluid.

While you turn open the can, upend, dump contents into pot
and light the flame way to high,
I stare at your body and neck.
You are crystalline in how tidy your studio is,
how organized your drawers,
how clean each key on your typewriter.
Converse, I am softened liquid water
as full disorganized as our tinned food
like pieces of myself disassemble
in any moment, trail behind me guilty.
As you cook you wait for me to freeze over
so we can go out. At a loss
you coat me in Paris,
slap a bow-tie on me.
Hang on my arm like you are expensive, hang me off yours
like I am concrete built of pearls.
Adjust everything until it is just right
and I won't feel ridiculous,
in your garrote like polka-dots
that aren't even clipped on no not ever a clip-on.
Won't feel ridiculous in the slightest.

No. 625.
Bruises—How Cured.

You disguise your injuries.
Cover them with planks. Lie like planks lie
spread by means of a brush.
Cover your whole body with wood
and cover wood wholly with the preparations.
This will make part of a white color,
something we can later flake off
gather like snow at ankles
wood covered which turn to matchsticks
where your toes normally would be
spread by means of a brush.
Pressure will be also of service, heavy, quiet,
instead of a blue or greenish yellow
only the purgatory white flakes off the knives
spread by means of a brush.
When you aren't looking I knock
lightly on your shoulder as if something
might answer, come out, invite in.
Forever later I ask if we can take away the wood;
you blink shingle eyes and say
you no longer know what's beneath
you or nothing or otherwise
such as marble or ivory or steel
each and all spread
by means of a brush.

No. 752.
A Good Baking Powder.

As boys I say we will throw acid at each other
eventually. It is inevitable.
You say you like the way the word rolls
out of my mouth when I'm wasted. Inevitable.
8 ounces.
We color each other's pages without asking
outside the lines and pull hair
scrape our knees from kneeling,
cut at hearts, unfold them to snowflakes,
drop them on each other, wait for them to melt.
9 ounces.
Still young, you move to Belgium. I don't. I don't
think it's a real place. Belgium. There are borders
to our world that we built and they are small but absolute.
I think you are moving just to
prove me wrong about all this.
You prove me wrong.
You come back with the chocolates.
10 ounces.
You say you came back for me.
I say you just got bored.
This is how we fight,
A series of negations
like we are trying to talk the other
out of existing.
You are rigid like if you were to hit me

but you don't know how to hit me
you never hit anything. You are so tired and crying
wet, soaked through angry so I can
smell the adrenaline.
11 ounces.
We do not put our walls back up around us, instead
let the world seep out sand from a broken box.
Your eyes burn like when we're in bed.
But we're not in bed.
I say I told you so.
Quiet, so only you can hear me.

INDEX

Acknowledgments

To my editors Diane and Lily and everyone at Black Lawrence Press who've shepherded this and my previous book through the process, thanks for your patience, and belief. And my family as always.

This project was started in the Poble-sec neighborhood of Barcelona in a tiny café across a table from Kiely Sweat. None of this would have come about without her continuous support and encouragement. There are few people in the world as loving and kind.

And to all the poets in New York, including but by no means limited to Amy, Monica, Ryan, Paige, Sam, Bianca, Angelo, Christine, Veronica, all the many, many Bens, thanks for all the parties, the brunches, the writing retreats that were mostly cocktails, and the never-ending readings that always contained at lest one moment of pure inspiration.

Notes / Previous Publications

Each of these poems is an adaptation of a recipe found in *The Standard Cyclopedia of Recipes* published in 1901 by Frederick J Drake and Company.

The title of each recipe is an exact duplicate of the source material.

Thanks to the original author, Chas. W. Brown, for inspiring this project with the strangest book I've ever read.

Some of these poems have been previously published (possibly in a different form) in the following journals. Many thanks to the fantastic editors at:
La Petite Zine; No, Dear; Freerange Nonfiction; Lyre Lyre; Food-i-Corp

The second section, *To Mend Small Children*, was published (in a slightly edited form) by Augury Books. Love to Kate and Christine for their help and all the wine.

B.C. Edwards was raised in Newburyport, Massachusetts. He is a producer at the Upright Citizens Brigade Theater and attended the Graduate Writing Program at the New School in New York City. In addition to this, he is the author of a collection of short stories, a chapbook of poetry and several essays. He lives in Brooklyn.